# *Flower Storms on the Riverbank*

### By

# Preeti Kulkarni

*Flower Storms on the Riverbank,* Published October, 2020

Editorial and proofreading services: Highridge Editorial, NY, NY; Karen Grennan
Interior layout and cover design: Howard Johnson
Illustrations: Jasmine Smith

Photo Credits: Author photo: © Rainbow Images
Illustrator photo: © Russell Smith

 **SDP Publishing**

Published by SDP Publishing, an imprint of SDP Publishing Solutions, LLC.

ISBN-13 (print): 978-1-7343317-9-0

Library of Congress Control Number: 2020916697

# For My Mom, Swati Kulkarni

*Thank you for holding me in the late hours of the night, and for giving me a head massage whenever I need it. Thank you for loving me unconditionally, when I howl with aggressive laughter when you're trying to work. Thank you for teaching me how to dream and dream big. This book is for you and all of the fearless mothers who would climb to the top of Mount Everest to make their child's dreams come true. The love I have for you is endless. Thank you very much.*

# TABLE OF CONTENTS

# *2*
# THOUGHTS 57

# *3*
# VIGNETTES 69

# *4*
# EMOTIONS 79

# 5
# EXPERIENCES 101

# From Me to You

Dear reader,
This,
This book,
That you're holding,
Right now,
Either with a cup of double espresso coffee on a Sunday morning,
Late at night when you can't fall asleep,
Or even,
When you feel like no one understands you,
When you feel like everything has crumbled,
And you only have yourself,
And your 'sad music' playlist on Spotify.

I,
The author,
Am here to tell you that,
You
Have my diary.
You
Have the key to my soul.
You
Have my emotions on paper.

You
Mean so much to me.
You
Are not alone.
No matter what you're going through right now,
You have me.

We
Can be vulnerable
Together.
We
Can ride this crazy rollercoaster called 'life'
Together.
We
Can paint the town red
Together.
We
Can make memories
Together.
We
Can be the best of friends.

This book
Connects us,
Through good and bad.
Through love and heartbreak.
Through success and failure.

This book
Is me.
You have me.
We are connected.
We are one.

# The Purpose

Instead of
The typical
"About the author"
Paragraph,
I'll just tell you about me
The way I know best.

Hi,
My name is Preeti Kulkarni.
I'm fifteen years old.
This is my first book.
I'm kind of nervous.
People say that my writing,
Is beautiful,
Is out of this world,
Is tear jerking,
Is real.

Do
You think so?
I mean,
Your opinion matters most.
You're the reader.
It's your job
To critique my experience.
It's your job
To approve of my work.

I'm glad you enjoy it if you do
Reader.

These are my emotions
Reader.
This has been my life
For two years
Reader.
Hours and hours
Have gone into this
Reader.
This has been my release
Reader.
A place where I'm completely honest
Reader.

And since I'm completely honest here
Reader,
I
Have a piece of advice for you
That I have learned in my fifteen years of life.

You,
Dear reader,
Should stop caring
About what people think about you.

There will always be something
That someone will say about you.
There will always be something
That someone will think about you.

You
Being yourself
Is so much more likeable.
You
Being authentic
Is so much more aligned with what life is all about.
You
Being real
Is something that is beyond
A lot of people.

This book has helped me find myself,
And I hope it helps you too.
This book has helped me love myself,
And I hope it helps you too.

# 1

# RELATIONSHIPS

# You and I

I
In my red, silk, lehenga,
Embroidered with hopes and excitement,
Each bead is full of content.

I
Walk closer to the mandap.
My bangles tinkle shyly.
My anklets jingle a sweet song of anticipation.
My makeup can't hide the cherry red blush on my cheeks thinking
of you.

The palace is twinkling.
The sky is dancing.
The souls of our ancestors are smiling.
The eyes of our family fill with tears.
The gods up there grin.
A match made in heaven.

You
In your shining, golden kurta.
Each speck of gold is singing tunes of peace.
Each thread is painted by love.

You
Hold my hand as we sit together,
In front of the Agni.
Your eyes,
Speak a thousand words by tears.
Your smile,
Spreads our love across this painted sky.

The palace is twinkling.
The sky is dancing.
The souls of our ancestors are smiling.
The eyes of our family fill with tears.
The gods up there grin.
A match made in heaven.
We
Walk out of the palace,
Hand in hand,
And gaze into each other's eyes.

You
Kiss my forehead.
I
Rest my head on your shoulder.

Our lives are now one.
Our souls are now one.

We are now one.

# Words of My Mother

There are many rocks,
And there are a couple diamonds,
But there is only one Kohinoor.

Everyone knows it.
Everyone wants it.
Everyone worships it.

If the Kohinoor cries about its loneliness,
There is no need for consolation.
Yes, it is lonely.
Yes, it is isolated,
Because it's one of a kind.

# My Dear Mentor

As you sip your chai,
On a Sunday morning,
Your aged hands tremble as you attempt,
To pick up the china cup.
Your eyes stare blankly at the portrait on the wall.
I guess you're thinking.
"What are you thinking about, Anna?"
I ask eagerly.

You snap out of your elderly daze,
And stare lovingly back at me.
"Oh, nothing dear. I was just thinking."
Your eyes seem to well up with tears,
While looking at me,
In my casual Sunday morning attire.
"You. You are a God-gifted girl."
Your eyes sparkle as you say that.

Your deep blue eyes.
I can see a lifetime in them.
Your deep blue eyes.
They reveal all of your innermost feelings,
If you look at them for long enough.

To you, my eyes sparkle.
To you, I bring such joy.
To you, I have the light of God,
Waiting to grow in me,
Like a tiny plant,
That blossoms,

And blossoms,
And blossoms.

You are right.
I am a God-gifted girl.
I am a God-gifted girl because,
I have a mentor like you.
I have a friend like you.
I have a confidante like you.
I have a grandfather like you.

Whatever I do in life,
Is all thanks to you.
Whoever I become,
Is all thanks to you.
Who I am today,
Is all thanks to you.

Thank you, Anna.

# I'm In Love with Myself

I stare longingly out the window.
The ocean is crashing on the beach floor.
The sun starts ascending.
The sky looks like a painting.

I stare longingly out the window.
The clouds blend into the sky.
The warm air seeps through the window.
It embraces me.

I stare longingly out the window.
The sky and the ocean are the same color.
The sun is shining so bright.
The light kisses my face.

I smile from ear to ear.
I close my eyes and let the happiness sink in.
This is independence.
This is the freedom I've wanted for myself,
For so long.
This is the love I've needed for myself
For so long.

# Love Wrapped into a Masala Dosa

You know,
Saturday mornings are my favorite part of the week,
When you're around.
They feel different when you're around.

I wake up to the smell of sandalwood and chai.
I wake up to the sound of your bangles.
They're calling out to me.
I wake up to the sweet and tender stroke of your hand
across my forehead.
"Wake up beta".
You say that with so much love.

As I slowly open my eyes,
I see your face,
Staring back at me.

Although weary,
Although tired,
Although pained,
Although aged,

Your face still has a glow.
It has so much life left in it.
Your eyes,
The wooden brown of them is,
So warm,
So comforting,
So real.

Your smile,
Is filled to the brim,
With unsaid words,
And unheard laughter,
And hidden happiness.

I get out of bed and quickly freshen up.
The smell of breakfast echoes throughout the house,
Urging me,
Tempting me out of my humble room.

I gently walk out of the bathroom,
To see you,
Hard at work in our humble kitchen.

You mingle with the spices.
You gossip with the utensils.
The kitchen is a safe haven for you.
The food you make,
Has a different taste.
The only way to describe it would be heavenly.
The only way to describe the ambience you create
is full of love.

You know,
Saturday mornings are my favorite part of the week,
When you're around.
They feel different when you're around.

You make it so special.
You make it so warm.
You make it so familiar.
You are a blessing in the disguise of my grandma.
You are my everything.

Thank you for loving me so much.

24

# India

Whatever I am today,
Whatever I am today and whatever I will be in the future.
Is because of the roots that keep my feet cemented to the ground.
Is because of that warrior blood rushing through my veins.
Is because my tongue is painted with different languages.
Is because my life has been painted with difficult experiences.
Is because of the values I hold as second nature.
Is because I hold India and America in my heart.

Whatever I am today,
Whatever I am today and whatever I will be in the future,
Is because I never forgot my ancestors.
I never forgot my culture.
Even though,
America is my residence.
The fresh smell of roti and the Indian soil,
Is my home.

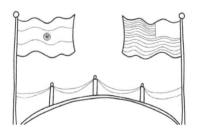

# Like Peanut Butter and Jelly

I text you at 10:30 at night.
You answer.
I cry on your shoulder.
You comfort me with our stupid jokes.
I vent.
You listen.
8 years,
You've seen my whole life,
And I've seen yours.
You've stuck by me
And I promise to stick by you.
I can tell you anything
I trust you
I love you
Thank you, best friend.

# Three, Two, One

You fear that I will replace you,
Yet you replace me every day.

You vent to me about how you feel excluded,
Yet you don't even try to be included.

You say you hate your life.
I hate seeing you cry
I want to help you,
And love you,
And be your best friend.

But everything I do and say
Is a ticking time bomb,
Waiting to burst and end.

# Someone to Be Determined

I am in love with everything you do.
Your goofy smiles,
Your howling laughter from across the hall,
The stupid hand holds,
The comforting hugs,
Your inquisitiveness,
Your intelligence,
Your happiness,
Your kindness,
Your annoying sense of humor.

You're the only guy that has treated me well.
You're the only guy who
Hasn't hurt me,
You made me feel again.
You're my best friend.

I have never felt as safe as I do around you.
I feel free around you.
I feel comforted around you.
Whenever a stupid love song comes on the radio,
I think about you.
I smile at our adventures from the day as I drift off to sleep.

If you haven't gotten the memo,
I'm in love with you.
You're my first love.

# Blemish

As I stare off into space
Daydreaming of the day,
You would tell me you love me,
I immediately stop myself.

Why do I have to suffer like this?
I want your hug.
Your touch.
Your kiss.
Your love.
But
You gave it to her,
My best friend,
I can't even hate her for it.

I guess the happiness that she feels around you,
Isn't destined for me.
I guess feeling as free as she does around you,
Isn't destined for me.
I guess your love isn't destined,
For me.

# Friends

Friends are the ones who love you,
Not because you have money,
Or because you are popular,
Or because they want gossip.
They should love you,
Because you are you.

I'm lucky to have those types of friends.

# They Left Me Stranded at Sea and Tried to Convince Me I'm on Land

I thought our friendships would last forever.
I guess I'm easily replaceable.
I was so sad to leave you all,
And you forgot me in a second.

I'm alone.
Going to an unknown school.
With unknown people.
With a new unknown identity.

I thought,
No matter
Who I would lose,
Who would hurt me,
Whatever hurdles I would have to overcome,
I would have you guys.

I want you guys in my life more than ever.
How can you not see me?
I want to stay rooted to you all,
And you're the ones uprooting me.
You say we're best friends forever.
Yet, you're always too busy
for me.
Did you really want me
gone from your life?

# Empty Smiles

Why are you such a crybaby?
Whenever I get a taste of success,
You take it away by using,
Hurtful
Distasteful comments,
As your weapon.

Whenever I hold his hand,
I feel a piercing glare right through my heart.
I get shot down once again.
I loved him.
You can see it.
I loved him.
You took him from me,
And I stood there with a fake smile,
Drawn on my face by you.
You say you care.
You don't care.
Whenever you smile at me,
I feel hatred.
I thought you were my friend.

# My Second Mother

Thank you,
For being my second mother.
For sneaking out of the house and watching movies with me.
For buying me gifts for no reason.
For being there for me at my lowest.
For being so strong.
For being you.

You supported me when no one else did.
You understood me when no one else did.
You painted my life with an undeniable amount of happiness.

I cherish you,
And will love you,
For the rest of my life.

# Care

I love you so much,
And I want to thank you so much,
For bestowing knowledge.
For bestowing care.
For bestowing love,
On this little girl.

You comforted me in the late hours of the night.
You held me in your arms when I cried my eyes out.
You never yelled at me.
You never hurt me.
You appreciate me.
You told jokes with me.
You laughed with me.
You taught me.
But most importantly,
You loved me.
Thank you.

# I Learnt Love from You

You are my world.
We come in a package.
I couldn't imagine my life without you.
You listen to all of my stupid drama and complaints.
You give me advice when I don't want to hear it.
You're my life.
You're my comfort.
You're part of my soul.
You're helping me grow each and every day.
You're continuously molding me into,
An independent woman,
And I'm so grateful to be blessed with a mom
Like you.

But you are more than an amazing mom.
You are the most selfless person I know.
You are the epitome of a woman.
You are an inspiration.
You never break down in front of me,
Despite how much we have overcome.
You deserve all of the accolades and riches in the world.
Unfortunately, I can't give you any of that right now.
All I can give you is pride,
Which I hope I've given you.

Thank you for everything.

# The Hidden Poison

Fake friends,
The ones that pretend to love you.
Fake friends,
The ones that loathe fake people,
But end up sounding just like them.
Fake friends,
The ones that emotionally drain you,
But accuse you for no reason.
Fake friends,
The ones that say they miss you,
But don't actually.
Fake friends,
They replace you in a minute.
Fake friends,
You lost them but they're still smiling,
With people that you hate.

You said you wanted a best friend.
You said you wanted true friendship,
And I gave you everything you wanted.
But what did you give me in return?
Agony.
Just agony.
That's a fake friend.

# A Tear-Decorated Scrapbook

I miss the old you.
The one that brought me something with his first salary.
The one that left his date to buy me chocolate,
On Valentine's Day.
The one that taught me basketball.
The one that let me sneak into his bed at night,
And held me in his arms,
And told me everything was going to be okay.
The one that made tents so we could stay up,
All night,
And just talk.
The one that left sleepovers with his friends,
To have sleepovers with me.
The one who bunked homework,
To draw things for me.

I still have those drawings.
I love you more than words can describe.
Just please come back.
I need you more than ever.

# Just Stop

Stop lying,
Telling me that you love me.
You don't even know what love means.

Stop lying,
Saying that this mess wasn't your fault,
Because it was.

Depression?
Do you even know what that means?
Stop making me worried,
For no reason.

Depression?
Isn't solved by meditation.
It's solved by medication,
Which you don't need.

After countless
Blood pressure medicines,
Tooth surgeries
And depression meds,
You still pester me.
You still beg for me to help you.
But I receive no thank you or
I love you in return.
Stop asking me for pity
And start feeling love.

# Goodbye

Leaving you,
Is proving to be the hardest thing,
I've ever had to do.

I truly,
Deeply loved you.
But unfortunately, I have to let go.

I have to let go so that you can be happy again.
I have to let go so that I can be happy again.
I have to let go so I can leave you and not cry again.
I have to let go so I can move on again.
I have to let go to begin a new chapter in my life.
Again.

Leaving you,
Is proving to be the hardest thing,
I've ever had to do.

I truly,
Deeply loved you,
But unfortunately, I have to ignore you.

I have to ignore you so that I can free myself.
I have to ignore you so that I can better myself.
I have to ignore you, so I don't feel a stab,
Every time I look at your face.

The pain of leaving you is torture,
But the pain of staying would've killed me.

# Stabs

You're in pain.
I get it.
You crave attention.
I get it.
People miss you.
I get it.
You want the world to do your bidding.
I get it.

The thing is,
No one did that for me.
But I never complained.
I handled everything by myself.
I want the applause that you get.
You get everything that you want.
I earn things by hard work.
I'm a warrior of a girl.
You can take everything else away from me.
But you can't take my warrior spirit,
And you never will.

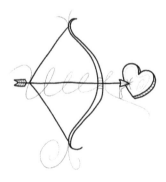

# One Final Hug and Goodbye

I feel like a bride on her wedding day,
Leaving her family behind.
Even though I will see you all,
It won't be the same.

These three years have been,
The best three years of my life.
Even through all of the very,
Very bumpy patches in the road.

You guys have joked with me like siblings,
Advised me like parents,
And showered me with love like grandparents.

We've made countless memories together,
and we'll continue making more.
We've broken so many molds,
and we'll continue breaking more.

You guys have a special place in my heart.
You guys are a part of my family.
You guys are a part of my story,
And I'm a part of yours,

And that's beautiful,
And I'll hold on to all of you,
'Til my very last breath.

# You're a Waste

My body is shaking,
Not with anxiety,
But with anger.

The threatening way,
You form your questions.
It seems like you want to eat every bit of sanity,
Left in me.

The way you caress my hand.
Get off my hand.
The way you caress my back,
And straighten it.
Get off my back.
The way you caress my head.
Get off my head.

Stop making me come to this hell hole.
Stop wasting my time.
Stop wasting my life.

# Rot in Hell

You.
You insatiable monster.
Because of what you thought was a joke.
People were scared for their lives.
I cried for my friend's safety,
Because she's so innocent.
More pure than dew sitting on a leaf.
She thinks you can't do anything.
Well,
I know exactly what you can do.

You.
You insatiable monster,
Trying to ruin my friend's life,
Chipping at it,
Piece by piece,
Turning all of her friends against her,
Making her a target,
Because of your stupidity.

Everyone thinks that you're innocent.
A wilted flower once pure but corrupted.
You don't have an ounce of innocence in your
Rotten heart.
I can never believe you.

You hurt her.
You hurt everyone.
I can never forgive you.
No one ever will.

# Thank You All for Everything

Sometimes,
I feel so trapped.
Like walls are closing in on me.
Like I'm in a straitjacket.
Like I'm stuck in a dark closet.
Like I don't have space to move.

Sometimes,
I feel so cold.
Like my fingers on a cold day.
Like my brain after a grueling test.
Like my heart has shut down.

Sometimes,
I feel so exhausted.
Like my legs will give out.
Like I will go limp.

It would be so much easier to keep all of this emotion inside.
It would be so much easier to be numb again.
It would be so much easier to be the old me.
It would be so much easier not to get better.

I have to get better however.
For the people who are rooting for me.
For the people who care.
For the people who listen.
For the people who love me.
For the hope that someday
I'll feel light again.
For the hope that I feel like me again.
I'm trying my hardest and always will for you all.

# First Blow of Betrayal

I really miss you.
Even though,
You disappointed me.
Even though,
I thought you had my back,
When you didn't.
Even though,
I thought you cared about me,
When you didn't.

Why haven't you talked to me in ages?
Why didn't you wish me on my birthday?
Why don't you find it necessary to check up on me?
Why didn't you comfort me when I cried my eyes out
trying to talk to you?
Why can't you see how much I need you?
Why?

# I Miss All of You So Much

I wish,
I wish we lived on Pangaea,
Instead of thousands of miles away from each other.

We would make countless memories.
We would laugh like maniacs.
We would listen to romantic songs,
And cry together.
We would walk together,
Hand in hand,
As the sun goes down,
And hug,
And smile,
Because we had each other.

I wish,
I wish we lived on Pangaea,
Instead of thousands of miles away from each other.

We could talk face to face.
We could be authentic.
We could be crazy.
We could be funny.
We could be dumb.
We could be us.

Our friendship is the same as every other friendship.
We're just talking through screens,
And are 3,678 miles away from each other.

Our friendship is as golden,
As valid,
As true,
As real,
As raw,
As if we were face to face.

# To the People I Love

You,
You are the definition of beauty.
You are like the sunshine on a cloudy day.
You leave me in awe.
You leave me speechless.

How could you be so kind?
How could you keep me so bright every day?

You,
You are the definition of beauty.
You're a light.
You shine so bright,
That everyone in your path has to stop and stare.

How do you inspire me every day?
How do you manage to make the worst day seem amazing?

You,
You are the definition of beauty.
You make winter seem like spring.
You make life seem like a game of tic tac toe,
Not chess.

You,
And your personality.
You,
And your shining smile.
You,
And your comforting light.

I'm so lucky to have you in my life.

# The Beginning of The End

Why?
Why are you doing this to me?
Cute pick-up lines and love one minute.
Cold responses and disdain the next.

Why?
Why are you doing this to me?
Why are you falling out of love with me?
I thought you cared.
You said you did.
I thought you loved me.
You said you did.

Why?
Why are you doing this to me?
You never seem to respond to me until hours later.
Do you even miss me?
You never make the first move.
Was this all a lie?
You rescheduled our plans four times.
Do you even want to see me?

You know,
You still plague my mind.
Oh, those sweet words.
Oh, those kisses.
Oh, those hand holds.
From a month ago.

Honestly,
I love you too much to leave you.
Otherwise I would've.

A long time ago.
I felt like a toy.
Is that what I am to you?
Am I just an option?

I'm bawling my eyes out right now.
We're taking things slow,
You said.
We're not even moving.

You don't understand,
How frustrating it is to be loved one minute,
And ignored the next.
You don't understand,
How frustrating it is to feel on top of the world,
And low at the same time.
You don't understand,
How frustrating it is,
To love you.

# On the Other Side

I aimlessly stare at the cafeteria wall
As I hear you.
Begging for attention.
Holding on to the little string of care that people give you.
You want my friends?
You can have them.
You want my talent?
You can have it.
You want my personality?
You can have it.

You want everything all to yourself.
But one day you'll realize,
How far you've run away from everything.
Your friends
Your abilities
Your core self
When all you needed to do was understand it.
When all you needed to do was be honest with it.
When all you needed to do was spend time with it.
When all you needed to do was love every second of it.

# Green with Envy

You're the villain to my hero.
My success is your failure.
I take pride in myself.
You aim to take that very pride
Away,
Aimlessly chipping away,
At my grandeur.
I'm at the top of my mountain.
Looking below,
At you,
Desperately trying to climb.
Trying and trying to reach me
But you can't.
You never will.
I get applause.
You get taunts.
Tell me who the winner is.

# Above the Clouds

When I'm with you,
I feel like I'm dancing on clouds,
Really puffy clouds.
The ones that cushion your thoughts
When you look up at the sky.
The ones that soothe you to sleep
When no other thought seems to work.
The ones that make everything better.

Our friendship
Is so unexplainable.
Our friendship
Is so simple yet so complex.
It's like a macaroon in a French bakery.
Sweet and soft,
Layered and well crafted.
It makes sense.
Our friendship is like chai on a rainy day.
It warms my soul to have
a friend like you.

# A Letter to Myself from 2018

Dear me from the past,
I just wanted to take a couple minutes of your time,
To help you understand how far you've come,
In this past year.

Last year,
You spent days and nights
Crying.
Tears soaked the carpet
Of the apartment you had just moved into.
Nightmares plagued your mind in the night.
Anxiety plagued your mind in the day.

The only things you thought you had were,
Your grades,
And your writing.
The only people you thought you could talk to,
Were your therapist,
And your mom.

Friends felt like strangers.
Family felt like betrayers.

You forgot who you were.

This book,
Was your soul.
This book,
Was your escape.
This book,
Cured you.

You're in high school now,
At the school of your dreams.
It was everything you hoped for and more.
It's like life was waiting.
Waiting for you to turn this corner,
So it could fill you up to the brim with happiness.
You have the best of friends.
You have the same bond with your family.
You're excelling in school.
You are doing so well.

I hope you realize that,
The tears were worth it.
The anger was worth it.
The sadness was worth it.
Your pain was worth it.

You have the world in your hands now.
Let's hope by next year,
You've used our new-found happiness
To do some good.

# 2
# THOUGHTS

# Ambition

Ambition,
A feeling for some,
A condition for me,
That has
Coated every bone,
Rebuilt every muscle,
Coursed through every vein
In my body with undeniable vigor.

Dreams,
That have turned into reality,
Due to this blissful condition.
Which has driven me to,

Success.
Oh what a sweet nectar.
When it hit my tongue,
It was as if
The world had dropped into my hands.

Strength,
Which has tagged along,
Has given me the power to
Take every tribulation,
And make it my stimulation.
Thank you,
Ambition,
For all that you have done,
For me.

# A Girl with a Dream

I'm a girl with a dream
I want to be successful
So successful that
No one would underestimate a girl ever again
As so many underestimated me

I'm a girl with a dream
I want to be at such excellence
Such caliber
That when I walk on a stage
The world freezes
And waits for me to address it

I'm a girl with a dream
I want to inspire
Inspire girls like me to have the desire
To dream big
To be the supreme court judge
To be the president of the united states
To be a businesswoman
To be a lawyer
To be whatever they please

I'm a girl with a dream
And that dream is
Passion
Ambition
Education
All things every girl has a right to.

# Pride and Freedom

I take in a deep breath.
The air is so crisp.
I love it.

The wind brushes against my shoulders,
And sits on them like powerful shoulder pads.

I walk into the room,
and it freezes.
A thundering wave of applause sweeps the room.

The ground beneath me,
Shudders in respect and slight fear,
Of my robust steps.

My shoes glide on the steps to the podium
Like a flowing river
And I start my address.

More than the tangible awards,
The chance to be free,
And express myself.

The chance to be a voice.
The chance to say.
The chance to add another
gleam to my mother's eyes.
That is the true reward.

# Childhood (Or Lack Thereof)

I'm not allowed to swear because I'm a child.
I'm not allowed to drive because I'm a child.
I'm not allowed independence because I'm a child.

If I'm a child and so small,
While the "adults" are grown and tall,
Why did I have to pick up your mess?
Why did I take care of everyone?
Why do I have to sacrifice my childhood?
Why did I have to be responsible?
Why did I grow up so fast?
If I'm a child and small
Why do I have to act like I'm all grown up?

# Egotistical Behavior

You think you work hard?
You think you're mature?

Try waking up at 5:40 a.m.,
Going on a four-mile run,
Coming home,
Legs throbbing,
Then getting ready to go to school.

Working your butt off like you always do.
Getting the highest grades like you always do.
Impressing teachers with your eloquent speaking,
And excellent writing.
Wowing everyone around you with your well versed
Opinions,
Goals,
And desires.

After all of this,
Go home.
Support your family.
Be your absolute best for them.
Care for them with your whole heart.

I'm still not mature?
I'm still not working hard enough?

Live a day in my life.
You'll regret saying anything.

# Crying a River

Please don't cry,
Not right now.
That would cause a lot of unnecessary issues.

Please don't cry.
I know you hate this but
It'll be over soon.

Please don't cry.
You've always been on your own.
Why is this situation any different?

Please don't cry.
I know you feel lonely.
You feel unwanted.
You are in a constant state of,
"Why am I so sad?"
"Why am I so mad?"
And it's absolutely destroying you.

I know how you feel,
But
Please don't cry.
They don't care anyway.

# What's Your Problem?

I'm sick of your attitude.
I'm sick of the way you disregard me.
I'm sick of the way you try and "one up" me.
I'm sick of the way you twist my emotions.
I'm sick of the way you pretend to love me.
I'm sick of the way you pretend to be the victim.
I'm sick of the way you don't care about
anyone else besides yourself.

I'm sick of the way you twisted him against me, too.
I'm sick of the way you trapped him in a jail
composed of you and only you.
I'm sick of the way that both of you deny my existence,
care, and love.

What's your motive?
What's the point?
I thought I could trust you.
I guess I was wrong.

# Responsibilities

Responsibilities,
I want to run away from them.
Responsibilities,
I have to fulfill them.
Responsibilities,
They're a weight I can't seem to lift off.
Responsibilities,
They plague my mind
From the minute I wake up
To the minute I fall asleep.
Responsibilities,
They always find a way to drain me.
Responsibilities,
Are the strongest barrier
Standing between me
And my dream.

If responsibilities could move out of
the way,
Just for a little,
I would be able to reach the stars.
I would be able to touch the sky
And see the world from above.
I would be able to leave this hamster
wheel of daily life.
I would be able to achieve my purpose.

# OCD (perfectionism)

You can't feel happy right now.
No, that's not acceptable.
You got a B on that French test.
You haven't exercised in weeks.
You haven't done anything at all.

How dare you do nothing at all?
How dare you let yourself become a lazy slob?
Everything is falling apart.

Your grades aren't perfect.
You're unfit.
You're bad at everything.
And you're the farthest thing from perfect.

So how can you be happy if you're not perfect?
How can you be acceptable when you're not
Perfect?

The answer is,
You can't be anything if you aren't perfect.

# 3

# VIGNETTES

# Handcuffs

The last time you hugged me was when I was four years old. I vividly remember that day. It was bright like the sun had descended and crept into our little home. You had picked me up and swung me around your back like a tiny backpack. We ran out of the house. We went on our little adventure.

And when I fell, you scooped me up in your hefty arms. I thought you were my superman. I thought you would protect me no matter what came my way. I thought that you would be my rock. I thought that I could count on you. I thought you loved me.

From then on, our fairy tales and adventures had begun to disappear. I used to wait by the door for you to come home from work. You didn't even look at me. You just plopped your bag right next to me and started your evening ritual of sitting in the "family" room and watching television for who knows how long. I would run to your side and hold you tightly. You took my arms off of you and told me to leave you alone.

I had just started school then. The other kids made me feel that they didn't want me. I tried to tell you about my day. I tried to talk to you. I tried so hard to get you to notice me. I guess you didn't want me either. Circumstances ripped our relationship apart like it was a piece of paper. Some say if I was a boy, you would understand me more. It was the difference between a boy and a girl that broke us. Some say I'm too quick to judge your actions. Some say that you were the problem.

Most of the time, I don't know if I should miss you. Most of the time, I don't know if I should hate you. Most of the time, I don't know what to feel about you.

The blood that we share is like handcuffs. No matter how hard you try, you can't get free of them. When I saw your face, I felt a pounding pain in my chest. When I heard your voice, my head split with sharpness and torment.

My mind plummeted into a dark tunnel that is so hard to escape. I felt suffocated. It was hard for me to breathe. All I could think to do is cry.

Nowadays, seeing you is no less a chore for me than washing the dishes or cleaning my room. We are no more than strangers. We no longer hug. We no longer talk. We look aimlessly at each other not knowing how to interact. We just stare at the broken toy our bond has become.

Unfortunately, you can't put in new batteries to kick-start our relationship. Unfortunately, there is no superglue that can piece a shattered bond back together. I'm sorry that there is no quick fix for what has already been ruined, shattered, and discarded. Even now, I am still trying. Even though my anger for you is deeper than the depth of the Grand Canyon, I still love you. You couldn't hold me when tears were flowing out of my eyes onto my pillow like a flooding river crashing onto dry land. You couldn't care about me. You couldn't talk to me without screaming. You couldn't go a day without pointing out my faults.

However, I'm truly grateful for your presence in my life. You taught me how to be thick-skinned. You made me stronger than I ever thought I would be. You made me independent. You taught me how to stick up for myself and the people I love.

In a very painful and unintentional way, you shaped and grew me. I don't need you to pick me up anymore. I can walk on my own. I don't need you to teach me anything anymore. I've learnt it all myself.

People say that the worst situations and the hardest struggles make the best people. You, in your own twisted way, made me the most capable, kind, and successful person I could be. I guess I broke out of your handcuffs after all.

# Thank You, Mama

**6:30 a.m.** I hear your voice urging me to leave my bed and start getting ready to go to school. I grudgingly get out of bed. I drag my feet in the direction of the bathroom as I silently wish to myself that I get my favorite cereal for breakfast or a free period waiting for me at school. Thirty minutes later, I come out of the bathroom spotlessly dressed. My uniform skirt crisp and ironed to perfection. My shirt neatly tucked in. I walk into the kitchen. There it is. My favorite cereal. Sure, it has some protein cereal mixed in but I'm happy nonetheless. After looking at your face, I notice you look more tired than usual. Your eyes are aching for rest. I wonder if you got enough sleep last night. I wonder if you stayed up late glued to your work. I wonder what happened when my eyes were glued shut.

**12:00 p.m.** It's time for lunch. Today, I'm missing you more than ever. I don't know why. I guess it's because I'm scared. I guess I'm paranoid that all of the good things until now would end. I really like my new school. I really like my new friends. I really like this. I'm just afraid that the happiness that we built together will wash away. You've been my stable base in my building of happiness. No matter what happened, you've been a constant in my life. I guess I've never realized that until now.

**3:30 p.m.** I finally see you. After a long day. You seem to have missed me as much as I missed you. I see that you're stressed. I see the worry that you try and conceal with a loving smile. You seem to forget all of your daily worries and eagerly ask me about my day. Unfortunately, I can only say an

"It was fine, mom" before going on my phone in the car on the way home. I guess I couldn't tell you how much I missed you. I guess I was too tired to form words at that moment.

6:00 p.m. Tea time. My favorite time of the day. The warm smell of chai spreads across the room like a comfy blanket. I slowly sip my chai as I finish my homework or get ready for basketball practice. Your eyes are practically closed at this point. However, somehow you muster up whatever little energy you have in you to take me to practice. Even though your head is pounding, you let me blast music in the car because you know it helps me focus. Thank you for everything. I don't know what I'd do without you.

11 p.m. As I lie awake in bed, processing my day, I stumble on the same question as I did all day. Why were you so tired? Little did I know, you woke up as soon as the grocery store opened to get my favorite cereal even after staying up to finish that presentation for work. I don't know how you do it. I don't know how you could balance me and work.

Keeping you as an example, I try to work as hard as I possibly can. You've built me. You've molded me like clay. You taught me what love is. You taught me how to be myself. You let me explore. You understand me better than I understand myself. Your smile brightens my day like a ray of sunshine seeping into the window on days when I can't seem to wake up on time. Your presence makes all of this unruly change much calmer.

I guess the smell of protein powder waffles is what keeps me grounded. I guess seeing everyone keeps me happy. I guess watching Bollywood movies throughout the weekend is what keeps me connected to what comforts me most. I wouldn't have any of it without you. All of the blessings. All of the successes. All of the lessons. I wouldn't be me without you.

# Preeti (A Vignette)

Preeti sounds like a chirpy parrot, always talking, always laughing, always cheery. Preeti means love. Preeti means the light in a dark tunnel. Preeti means joy. Preeti is a smile. Preeti is a bright yellow, like the sun. It's the feel-good song on the radio that makes you want to dance. Preeti feels like India during Diwali, fun, loud, happy. My mother gave me this name. I guess she saw something special in me. I guess she thought I was the light in her tunnel. I guess as soon as she saw me, she thought of love. Whenever I think of love, I think of my friends that I love with all my heart. I think of my family that has supported me through thick and thin.

Preeti also means kindness. When I think of kindness, I don't just think of my friends or my family. I think of the small acts of kindness that I see every day. I can feel the warmth of a much-needed hug or even a compliment from a stranger.

Kindness and love are the main values of society. Kindness and love are what make a person whole. I wouldn't change my name because it would be like changing the most important part of me.

# Dear Dada

"If I make this shot, you can't have ANY of my Cheeto Puffs." That's what you said to me seven years ago. With all of the might in my 4'6" frame, I jumped and grabbed the ball. I saw the look of pride on your face. However, shortly after, I collapsed onto the cement driveway with a loud thump. My knee was an assortment of wounds of all colors. There was a moment of silence. My eyes began to well up with tears. I screamed louder than a police siren. I belted in pain and the only thing you could do as a 14-year-old boy was call for the closest adult around. Finally, our grandpa ran out of his humble rocking chair. He bolted out of the house. He paused when he saw me in your lanky arms, breathing with you and seemingly calm. After a while, he ran over to us and rubbed the alcohol swabs that I used to hate with a passion across my multiple cuts and bruises. I wailed. I kicked. I screamed. I had a tantrum. However, you held onto me with such protection. After a while, I had to stop. From that day on, I knew I could count on you. I knew that my older brother cared about me.

Years passed. We went from dress-up games to watching Netflix. We went from building science kits to talking about high school and life. We went through the ups and downs of growing up together. When everything was going wrong and no one could give me attention, you were right there. One night, when everything that was going on began to overpower my 7-year-old mind, I snuck out of my bed and quietly tiptoed into your room. You woke up right away, as if you knew I was there and scooped me into your arms before knowing what I was going to say. All you said was, "It's going to be okay, Preetu."

We were always there for each other. I was there for your first homecoming. You were there for my first piano recital. You read me your first essay. I read you my first poem.

77

I wish you weren't six hours away. Oh, I wish you were here right now. Can you believe it? I'm already in high school. I'll be going to my first homecoming in a month. You were right. High school is amazing.

Can I let you in on a little secret? Sometimes, when I really miss you, I touch the heart charm on my bracelet that's matching with yours. Somewhere, I feel like you get my message even though we're so far away.

You may not believe this, but you were one of the main reasons as to why I am who I am today. You taught me how to play basketball. You lifted me up when I was feeling less than graceful. You taught me how to always strive for the best in life. You made life so much easier. You and I were the most iconic duo.

I hope our relationship continues to be this way. I hope we continue to walk together as we did seven years ago. I hope that the race of life doesn't cause one of us to leave the other behind.

Oh, and if you didn't know this before, I love you.

# 4

# EMOTIONS

# Positive Thoughts

Insomnia
You bless me with running thoughts,
And blissful plots.
You bless me with time to reflect,
And project the world around me.
You bless me with loneliness,
And uncensored gracefulness.
You awaken my emotions,
And my thoughts,
That flow through my fingers,
Like a coursing river.
Although you seem like a curse,
You are indeed a blessing.

# The Pain You Can't Feel

Numbness
Is when you want to cry,
But tears don't flow out of your eyes.
Numbness
Is when your heart is shattered,
But you don't even feel a pinch.
Numbness
Is when everyone is beaming with happiness,
But you can only manage a sheepish smile.
Numbness
Is when pain doesn't exist anymore.
Is when hurt is daily routine.
Is when you want to say something.
You want to feel something,
But you can't,
Because you haven't had a feeling in
Days,
Weeks,
Months,
Years,
Decades,
However long.
You forgot what it's like to truly cry,
And truly laugh,
And truly live.
Numbness is a curse
To say the least.

# Quite Numb

When you gave me that high-five,
My hand felt
Numb.
You electrocuted me with your touch.

When you smiled at me,
My heart
Dropped
Out of my chest.
My mind was yelling at me,
Frantically,
Trying and trying,
To pick up those bandages
That were once on my heart.
Just a smile of yours
Revived my wounds,
Yet I couldn't feel a thing.

Love isn't pain.
Love is being numb to pain.

# Anxiety

My body is shaking,
An earthquake rushing through my bones.
My eyes are tearing up,
Dropping down like rain,
Tap dancing on the floor below me.
My brain is fogging up.
My thoughts block my path.
My heart goes numb.
Is this what collapsing feels like?

# Lonely

I take the long way home,
Where all the couples meet.
A sweet teenage romance blossoms every other day.
Everyone has a person.
Everyone is loved.
Except me,
For I am an outlier.

I am smart and witty,
Which isn't something boys find pretty.
I wear loose clothing and have short hair.
I could beat any guy in a push-up contest.
But that obviously doesn't make me the best.

I stare at them.
I just want a hug,
A warm smile,
A hand hold,
Stupid jokes and sweet kisses,
And a hint of love.
Why don't I have a person of my own?

# The Thoughts of an Optimist

The way our face looks can change someone's life
Could push them over the edge
Or could make their day.
Why waste your face on a frown
When you can use it for a beautiful smile.
Why hate
When you can love.

# Dried Up

No matter how many times I tried to not care.
No matter how many times I tried to forgive you.
No matter how many times I put you before me,
Even though you never deserved it.

I still feel my heart drop whenever someone mentions your name.
I still feel that missing piece of my heart that was supposed to be
for you.
I still feel broken whenever I have to see your face.

I wish you hugged me when I needed it.
I wish you were there when I needed it.
I wish you didn't only think about yourself.
I wish you took the time to understand me.
I wish you cared about me.
I wish you loved me.

It's been a year since that fateful day.
The place where I was once captive still feels like a prison.
Your presence is still daunting.
I still feel the same.
I just wanted time.
I wanted to forgive you.
But you didn't let me.
I wanted to get better.
You're not letting me.

Now my heart is crumbling.
It's like the desert.
Dry.
Broken.
Colorless.

Every desert has an oasis.
Where it's pleasant, happy, and alive.
I guess my oasis dried up too.

Why don't you tell me how to revive a desert with no oasis?
Why don't you tell me how to revive a shattered heart
with no hope?

# Pain from the Inner Depths of Your Soul

Depression,
Is when you try to be happy,
So desperately.
But you can't anymore.
Is when you try and get out of bed.
But you can't anymore.
Is when you try to brush your feelings,
The little ones you have,
*Off.*
But you can't anymore.
Is when you want to love.
But you can't anymore.

You can't do anything anymore.
You're numb and broken.
You're dead inside.
You can't revive yourself to try again.
You're done.

Depression ruins you
Kills you
And tortures you all in one blow.
And the worst part is,
By the time you realize what's
happening,
You don't even feel it.

# The Great Escape

Run!
Run as fast as you can.
This is your chance to escape.
Everyone's problems add a weight
On your shoulders.
If you don't leave now,
You're going to break.

Run!
Run as fast as you can.
Nothing will compare,
To the despair,
You're retreating from.
The stress is sticking to you like gum.

Run!
Run as fast as you can.
The wind is blowing in your face.
You feel alive.
You don't dwell.
The pain is a distant memory.

# Heartbreak (I Can Barely Even Feel Anymore)

I'm sitting here,
Writing angry poetry,
Questioning my life and everything about it.

I'm sitting here,
Writing angry poetry,
Fake smiling and laughing like everything's okay.
Nothing's okay.

I love him okay.
Stop judging me okay.
I can't help it okay.
I am jealous okay.
This is eating at my brain okay.

I wanted rain showers,
And pretty flowers.
An awkward moment,
Followed by a rushing energy current,
And an electric kiss,
Not caring about circumstances or rules,
It would've been perfect.

None of that happened
and none of it ever will.

# Love Has All the Power in the World

Love
Is the most confusing feeling in the world.
It breaks you,
And puts you back together.
It gives you unimaginable pain,
And immeasurable happiness.

Love
Is definitely blind.
Because it doesn't see society.
It doesn't see religion.
It doesn't see race.
It only sees the soul,
And how pure it is.

Love
Is a universal truth.
Every scripture,
Be it the Bible,
Or the Bhagavad Gita,
Mentions it.
Everyone feels it,
Young and old.

Love
Is an unsolvable puzzle.
Scientists couldn't solve it.
Philosophers couldn't solve it.
Hell, even Einstein couldn't solve it.

But what I know about love,
Is that love,
Although confusing,
Is the most powerful feeling in the world.

A hug can heal a thousand wounds.
A compliment can douse the sting of a thousand bullies.
A handshake can save lives.
Love can win against anything coming in its way
if we let it work its magic.

# True Love

Every time I see him,
My stomach gets all fluttery.
My mouth forms an instant grin.
My hands get jittery.
I can't form words.
I lose all of my senses.

Every time he hugs me,
I feel so warm.
I feel giddy.
I feel comforted.
I feel loved.

Every time he smiles at me,
My heart skips a beat.
My cheeks turn bright red.
Love songs play in my head.
The flowers look a bit prettier.
My poems flow better.
I can't stop writing about him.

Today,
He asked me to hang out.
My mind paints a beautiful picture
Of our perfect day.
Sweet talks and even sweeter laughs.
Memories being engraved into my mind.
A perfect day with him.

I fall even more hopelessly in love.
I'm so in love with him,
That he's the reason I smile.
That I feel better because of him.
No matter where life takes us.
No matter what we are.
I'll still love him just the same.

# Will You Come Again Next Year?

Love is like summer.
It's warm.
It's relaxing.
It's beautiful.
It feels like a dream.
It makes the world seem like heaven.

But like summer,
Love ends.
And when it does,
You feel empty.
You feel like your soul left your body.
You feel your heart break in two.
Your heaven disappeared.
It's all gone.

Now, you have to go through the seasons
Hoping for summer to come back.
Now, you have to find the
beauty in the other seasons
Just as you did with summer.
Now, you have to get used to
your new normal.

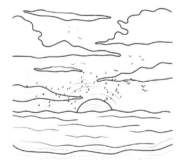

# Weird Place

I'm lost,
Dazed,
And confused.

I feel everything,
And nothing,
At the same time.

Lately, everything has felt like a game.
Relationships are being toyed with.
Emotions are being disregarded.
Words are being thrown at me like a ball.
What did I do to you?
Why did you say that?
What emotionally gratified you in that moment?

Lately,
Everything imaginable has been happening to me.
I want to cry but I can't anymore.
Nothing has been peaceful.
Not there, not here.
Circumstances wear me thin.

I'm lost,
Dazed and confused.
I don't know where life is heading,
And I'm scared for what's next.

# Mental Exhaustion

I constantly feel like crying.
I constantly feel like I'm drowning.
I constantly feel like my world is collapsing.

I try and try,
To pick up all of the pieces,
To fix everything in my reach,
To be my best at all times.

My mind is weary.
My heart is numb.

I'm just exhausted.

# I Am Quite in Love with You Huh

How to know if you're in love

Step one.
You feel his hugs.
You feel his presence even through a screen.
You feel him.

Step two.
Your mind is plagued by him.
Whether it's math class.
Whether it's the minutes before you fall asleep.
Whether it's when you first wake up.
He has made a little home in your mind,
That he can't seem to vacate.

Step three.
You love the little things about him.
You love the fact that he can't dance.
You love the tiny dimples that show up on his face
whenever he sees you.

So that's it.
How to know if you're in love.
To put it frankly,
You feel on top of the world.
You feel every feeling and you
cherish every second of it.

# 5

# EXPERIENCES

# School Shootings

As I wait in these dimmed locker rooms
I wonder about the possibilities
Will it happen to us?
All of the people that I've grown to love
Will they be taken away from me?
The school I've spent three years in
Will it be blown to pieces?

Well, everyone and everything goes at some point.

# Pollution of Society

I remember it like it was yesterday.
I was getting water.
He was walking.
My body tenses up.
He had said some things a couple hours before.
He asked me to
Stay after school.
I replied with a sharp blow of anger.
I know why he asked that question.
He mistook my kindness,
As my weakness.

When he saw me,
He froze,
And I froze.
Time had stopped.
He inched toward me.
I screamed.
I yelled.
I kicked.
I ran to the office,
And I filed my first complaint.

Harassment is an issue,
Not an isolated incident.
It's an epidemic,
A pollution of society,
And it stops,
Now.

# Equality

I'm not supposed to be here.
I'm a racial minority.
I'm not supposed to be here.
I'm the child of an immigrant.
I'm not supposed to be here,
Yet I am.

The fact of the matter is,
I am here.
I am excelling.
I am succeeding.

My identity stood the test of time.
My identity stood the test of strife.
My identity is winning.

However,
That fact of my life,
Isn't a universal truth.

A girl deserves equal opportunity.
An immigrant deserves equal opportunity.
Any person of color deserves equal opportunity.
Everyone deserves equal opportunity.

Why don't we have
equal opportunities?

# Leaders

Leadership,
Is when you speak,
And people follow.
But they don't just follow,
They listen and follow.
They understand your intentions,
And how your guidance can lead them,
Across dimensions of success.

Leadership,
Is when you tell a story.
A story people can resonate with.
A story told by numbers.
A story told by statistics,
You can make the most tedious report,
Sound like a fairy tale.

Leadership,
Isn't about being the ideal person.
It's about being authentic,
Being real,
Being understandable,
Being creative,
And being strong in your beliefs.

Leadership,
Isn't about pretty press conferences,
And glittering newspapers.

Leadership isn't about
Shaking the whole world with one bad decision,

Or creating controversies that could destroy a nation,
Or making people pawns,
Or being a dictator.

Leadership is about community,
It's about love.
It's about acceptance.
It's about understanding humanity.
It's about being a friend and a family member.
It's about bringing people together.

As I go on,
Onto bigger campuses and bigger dreams,
I will remember that I am a leader by giving.
I will remember that I am a leader by loving.

By that definition,
All of you are leaders too.
All of you have given me the strength to go on,
And I hope life will do the same for you.

# Gen Z: The Powerhouses

We are young, bright, and beautiful.
We have the world in our hands.
We can do anything.

We are young, bright, and beautiful.
We are in mutant stage of teen hood.
We want to conquer the world with our plastic swords,
And protect our rights
Safeguarding them with our youth.

We are young, bright, and beautiful.
We have so much potential.
And we are here to stay.

We are young, bright, and beautiful.
We know about gun control.
We protest.
We know about climate change.
We protest.
We know about gender inequality.
We protest.

We are young, bright, and beautiful,
And we are here to stay.

# I Thought You Loved Me

How?
How could you do this to me?
My tears fill up the floor.
My eyes are numb from crying.
My hands are shaking.
My mind starts spinning,
Round and round,
Round and round.

You stare back at me,
With an icy glare.
It pierces through me,
As you say those frigid words,
"You mean nothing to me."

How could you?
Of all people to say something so insensitive,
I didn't expect this of you.

# Oh My God

When I saw you for the first time,
My heart started beating out of my chest.
My mouth couldn't hold a straight face.
It burst into a grin.
My eyes were fixed on you like a moving target,
And my hands were shaking,
Like trees during a thunderstorm.

When I saw you for the first time,
I couldn't form words.
I could only blindly stare,
As you walked past me,
In the crowded hallway.
I fell in love right away.

# First Love Isn't Always a Fairytale

You are the subject of all of my petty jokes.
You are the crush that I regret most.
Not because I thought you were cute,
When no one else seemed to agree.

It's because you and your friends,
Broke me more times than one.
Your 'good guy' facade,
Had worked its charm.
A simple 'hi' or 'hello',
Would make my heart flutter.
A perfect time for you to cut it down.

You blushed,
When he yelled my locked-up feelings.
You were happy.
I saw the smile on your face.
I was a perfect target.

You and your friends made me a joke.
You and your friends attempted to make me a laughingstock.
But I didn't budge.
You see,
That warrior spirit in me,
Never let me stop moving.
That warrior spirit in me,
Never let me stop winning.

111

# A Dramatic Display of My Life

The blue-haired Cirque du Soleil performer,
Who glistened on stage.
Who touched my heart.
Who taught me how to feel again.

He caught me during the weirdest time.
You see.
I was shaking with anxiety the night before.
About new things.
And old pains.
I was gone.

Like me,
He had lost himself.
He was battling.
Light and dark.
Color and gray.
Happiness and sadness.
Numb and alive.

Like me,
He couldn't stand himself anymore.
He couldn't see the colors in his life.
He couldn't see anything at all.
He was blind to all hope.

I could feel a fire in him.
I could see my youth in him.
I could replay all of my memories with him.
I could connect to him.

For those two hours,
We were one.
For those two hours,
I felt comforted.
For those two hours,
My life was being played out on a stage,
And I could marvel at it.

He illustrated my life,
And I could finally understand it.

The blue-haired Cirque du Soliel performer,
Who glistened on stage.
Who touched my heart.
Who taught me how to feel again.

He taught me about life again.
He evolved with me.
He broke with me.
He lived with me.
He was me.

# The End

My tears sprinkle the sidewalk.
Drip drop.
Drip drop.
"Are you serious?"
My voice quivers when I spit out these
Cold,
Meaningless,
Words.

"Yeah I guess so."
Your voice is stern and confident.
I guess you're not in pain by this at all.
I guess you don't feel bad at all.
I guess this was all a game to you.

You know, I used to stay up late,
Painting thoughts,
About when I will see you again.
You know, I used to listen to love songs,
And you used to dance into my head and never leave
You never left.

You embrace me one last time.
I don't want to let go.
I never want to let go.
My tears soak your shirt.
Your cologne engulfs me.
Why?
Why do you have to leave?

The only thing I have left of you,
Is the sweatshirt you gave me on our first date.
The only thing I have left of you is,
The lingering smell of your cologne.
The only thing I have left of you is your imprint,
On my heart.
The only thing I have left of you is the past.

# The Process

Hurt.
I feel 1000 stabs
every time someone mentions your name.
I hate you with every bone in my body.
I will never forgive you.
You never cared about me.
I hate that in the little crevices in my heart,
I still care about you.

Breakdown.
I can't hold it in anymore.
A snarky lunch comment,
Triggered a tsunami,
Waves and waves of tears.
The cafeteria floor,
Damp.
I run to the bathroom stall.
I curl up into a ball.
I can only find comfort in myself.

Healing.
I feel better.
Even though,
Tears are still a part of my week.
Curling into a ball is still my only place of true security.
I'm still being pained.

At least I go to bed without soaking my pillow.
At least I can smile without crying on the inside.
At least I can feel without suppressing my pain.
At least I can find happiness in the small things.
At last I'm doing okay.

# The Ode of the Coronavirus

I have never missed my world,
More than I do today.

The sun shone brighter today.
Its light warming everything in sight.
Peeking through the window,
To brighten the view from my room.

The sky was a beautiful blanket today.
Its tapestry of clouds.
Its hints of pink,
Purple,
Blue,
And orange,
Swirling together,
Like a painting.

The grass looked greener today.
With little sprouts of flowers,
Waking up from their slumber,
In their ever so green,
Grassy bed.

The world looked like heaven today,
And I couldn't go outside.

I've never missed my friends,
More than I do today.
The echoing sounds of their laughter,
Rung in my ears.
The memories I made with them,
Replayed in my head like a movie.

The late-night stay ups.
The sudden breakfast plans.
The cart races at the top of the target parking lot.
All run through my mind as I twiddle my thumbs,
Looking out of my glass window.
Hoping,
Praying,
And waiting to see them soon.

Days are now spent,
Twiddling my thumbs,
Watching screens,
And going numb.

I wish this would all be over.
I wish I could go outside,
Lay on the grassy green bed,
And look up at the blanket sky,
And have the sun shine on my face,
With my friends by my side,
Laughing
Playing
Smiling.

I just want my life back.

# Thank You

This,
This is the end.
A year and a half,
Of creating,
Of crafting,
Of writing.

These
Emotions.
These
Words.
Would mean nothing,
Without,
You.

Poetry,
Is a special type of writing.
Poetry,
Can say so much in so little.
Poetry,
Can be anything.
Poetry is all around us.

Words are powerful.
Words are beautiful.
Words are freeing.
A picture may be worth a thousand
words.
But a word is worth a thousand
feelings.

This,
This is an end of a journey.
But I won't be done just yet,
I'm only fifteen.
I have plenty more to write about.

# Acknowledgments

First and foremost, my mother, Swati Kulkarni, who continues to encourage me and support me through all of life's trials and tribulations. My love for you is endless.

To my grandfather, Narayan Zalkikar, my grandmother, Meera Zalkikar, my aunt, Jyoti Zalkikar, and my cousin, Rahul Zalkikar, who have loved me unconditionally, who have continuously supported me through all of my doubts, fears, and goals, and who have taught me to find the best within myself. I love you all to the moon and back.

To my father, Prakash Kulkarni, who loved me unconditionally and taught me how to always strive for the best in life.

To my friends, for listening to me talk about this book for hours, and being the best friends I could ever ask for. I don't know who I would be without you all.

To Dr. Taranto, Mrs. Coon, Mrs. Anderson, and all other teachers I have had who inspired me to reach for the stars, and never let me give up. This book is a product of the determination you all have planted within me.

To Dr. Pereira and Dr. Mittal for giving me a safe space to express my emotions, and helping me understand them.

To my illustrator, Jasmine 'Jaszy' Smith, who believed in this project, and worked with me through every step of the way.

To my editors and publishers, HighRidge Editorial, NY, NY, and Lisa Akoury-Ross, who gave me guidance, support, and strength through the process of creating this book.

To the audience that gave me a standing ovation at my first open mic. Without you all, I would have never decided to pursue writing.

To my readers, who have now completed this journey with me. Your endless love and support mean the world to me.

# About the Author

Fifteen-year-old Preeti Kulkarni has been writing from a very young age. During a very tumultuous point in her life, she used writing as a safe space to express her deepest feelings, then ultimately deciding to embark on publishing her debut book of poetry. *Flower Storms on the Riverbank* was inspired by Rupi Kaur and other young Asian authors. Preeti hopes to be a similar voice for other young people, as those authors were for her.

# About the Illustrator

Jasmine 'Jaszy' Smith is a young artist from the coast of Mississippi. Jasmine has been drawing and painting her whole life and has been illustrating and painting murals full time since 2019. She thanks her husband, Russell, for encouraging her to follow her dream.

# Flower Storms on the Riverbank
## Preeti Kulkarni
Author website: preetikulkarni.com
Publisher: SDP Publishing
*Also available in ebook format*

 **SDP Publishing**

**www.SDPPublishing.com**
**Contact us at:** info@SDPPublishing.com

CPSIA information can be obtained
at www.ICGtesting.com
Printed in the USA
BVHW041305191120
R11489200001B/R114892PG593515BVX13B/4